OF DARKNESS & LIGHT

Of Darkness & Light

Poems by
KIM CORNWALL

Edited by
WENDY ERD

University of Alaska Press, Fairbanks

Published by
University of Alaska Press
P.O. Box 756240
Fairbanks, AK 99775-6240

Cover and interior design by Kristina Kachele Design, LLC

Cover image: *Across the Lake* by Sonia Cornwall (1919–2006). Kim's
great-aunt Sonia painted this watercolor thought to be a small lake near Sonia's
home on Jones Lake Ranch in British Columbia. Kindred souls, Sonia and Kim
shared an independence of spirit, a deep love of the rolling family cattle ranch
and a fierce commitment to their work, Sonia as painter, Kim as poet.

Photo of Kim and Spunky printed with permission of Arlene Cornwall.
Beluga Point photo from Wendy Erd.

Library of Congress Cataloging in Publication Data
Names: Cornwall, Kim, author. | Erd, Wendy, editor.
Title: Of Darkness and Light / poems by Kim Cornwall ; edited by Wendy Erd.
Description: Fairbanks, AK: University of Alaska Press, [2019] |
Identifiers: LCCN 2018031235 (print) | LCCN 2018032105 (ebook) |
ISBN 9781602233751 (ebook) | ISBN 9781602233744 (pbk.: alk. paper)
Classification: LCC PS3603.076856 (ebook) |
LCC PS3603.076856 A6 2019 (print) | DDC 811/.6dc23
LC record available at https://lccn.loc.gov/2018031235

I owe thanks to many for this publication of Kim's poems, most especially her mom, Arlene, for her tender graciousness and belief in this book; to Kim Stafford and Emily Wall for their insight, edits and encouragement; and to my husband, Peter Kaufmann, light of my days, who always cheers me on.

This book is dedicated to the luminous power of poetry and to Kim Cornwall, who lived poetry and whose laughter I can still hear.

You see, I want a lot.
Maybe I want it all:
the darkness of each endless fall,
the shimmering light of each ascent.
—*Rainer Maria Rilke* / The Book of Hours

CONTENTS

FOREWORD

and from silence and strange air
send a song

> *The most true thing to say is my poetry is a love response to the world.*
> *It's no different from a mother who hears her child say its first word, or*
> *someone who loves to cook making a masterpiece. Some things I'm very*
> *interested in expressing successfully in a poem are gratitude and wonder*
> *and survivorship. Alaska is filled, absolutely dense, with those things.*
> *In every poem I write, there is something about Alaska, and life here,*
> *in its genesis.*
> —KIM CORNWALL, interview in the *Anchorage Daily News*, 1997

I met Kim in 1996 in Homer, Alaska, at Gretchen Legler's memoir workshop. I thrilled to her writing soul. I had never read anyone's work at once so rich in language and unflinching. She was a fervent writer. She would write for hours to find the word. The line. She said she wrote with a "wildly grateful heart."

We shared a deep friendship and correspondence over the years. She had a kind spirit, an infectious laugh, and she believed in the beauty and power of poetry.

An intense desire to write brought the world into focus. She lived language. What little money she had she spent on poetry books, her bookshelves heavy with grace. Gleeful when she found a poet who thrilled her, William Stafford, Lorna Crozier, Dorianne Laux, Jane Kenyon, Naomi Shihab Nye and Mary Oliver became intimate friends of the heart.

Even as she was porous to the world with its small miracles, she carried a dark burden from childhood when as a young girl she was sexually assaulted on a field trip to a boy's boarding school. Her family, teachers and classmates were counseled, for Kim's sake, not to talk about it.

In all that ensuing silence, she wrote. Furiously and endlessly and beautifully.

> scars / are a Sanskrit we may never understand.
> ("Lungdhar [*Wind Flag*]")

We fired our own work back and forth. Poet friends. Nearly giddy at times, she poked fun at her obsession with perfection.

> I can't believe how much I can obsess over one word and its scary to reveal that to others [in our writers group] because I am afraid they will think I'm some kind of a nut for worrying so much. Of course what I want is for someone to tell me exactly what to do which is absolutely the wrong attitude. There are no easy answers are there to any questions we have about the things we fiercely love?[1]

If language was breath that buoyed her, love of Alaska sustained her.

Two decades after the brutal incident of her childhood, in the middle of the night she took off, driving from her family home in northwest Washington and with ferocious bravery returned to the boarding school to confront her memories and the school staff. Then, without destination, she fled north, driving to outpace what bound her.

She drove until she could drive no farther. In Alaska she lived for weeks in a tent on the beach until a new friend offered a cabin. As a woman on her own, she revived in such harsh beauty. Her new life was about survivorship.

And gratitude. And language.

She handed out poems by her favorite poets at the laundromat: an unabashed troubadour. She hosted poetry circles in an art gallery. She spoke of astonishment, of awe.

---

1 Personal email, February 2002.

> *It is all applause, / applause, applause. // How is it possible /*
> *to ask for more than that?*   ("Rough Drafts")

At times also struggling with depression, Kim recognized others in pain who had lost their way. She worked with challenged children in Homer. In Fairbanks she taught a poetry class for incarcerated youth going through tough times. She'd buy yellow gloves at a secondhand store, give one glove to each student and read them Naomi Shihab Nye's poem "Yellow Glove." In the poem a young girl bargains with life, secretly praying she'll be safe. Kim understood her students' challenges. She knew that narrow margin between "floating and going down,"[2] even as she deftly translated the world that came rushing in.

> *I am making my small stab at writing again. Began in short, unfruitful starts while I was there [in Homer] over Christmas and it has thrust me into a spiritual life again. Have all these small moments hurtling through me with personalized license plates dying to be read. It must show because a friend told me I have become radioactive in appearance.*[3]

In May 2002, at her great-aunt Sonia's cattle ranch in British Columbia, we climbed to a high meadow and lay in chuffy, uncut grass listening. Sprawled between the wide sky and the scratchy field, Kim told me then that at times life pulled her under, deep water dark down and without breath. She wasn't always sure she could surface. The next minute we heard a bluebird's song and she laughed, delighted. For Kim the world was unstoppable in its darkness and its light.

Later that day, I passed Kim near the empty corral on my way for a walk. She showed me a copper colored feather, a cone on a twisted branch, a handful of found treasure. As I wound up the hill she called after me, "Keep your eyes open. There's so much to see."

> *In the poem, the person is already awake. They're in a dark time, waiting for faith to begin, but they're active, awake—waiting and believing there is a song there.*[4]

---

2 From "Yellow Glove," Naomi Shihab Nye.
3 Personal email, January 2002.
4 Kim speaking of her poem "The Myth Makers" in the *Anchorage Daily News*, 2007.

Kim found ways to balance the darkness. Ever physical, with armloads of wood she stoked her woodstove: flames the autumn color of aspen trees outside her window. Joy rounded the bend of summer as she canoed Fairbanks's chill rivers. Slowly the scale swung though as unrelenting physical pain added to other challenges and eclipsed even her writing. In the summer of 2010, "in too much pain to feel much grace,"[5] she ended her life and left us, all too early.

This collection contains many of her unpublished poems. It is Kim's song to us all.

WENDY ERD

---

5 Personal email, June 2009.

LUNGDHAR (*WIND FLAG*)

In our final hour, we learn
the lesson of levity. Until then,
a prayer flag shifts in the wind. Maybe longing
is tethered to awe. We are all
flawed students of the same storm.
In peace, in grief, at war—
every hour is a new school.
When there are no headmasters left,
our seasons teach each other. Now,
fall berries stain our teeth, and scars
are a Sanskrit we may never understand.
You rise to the prayer you have,
thread by thread,
disappearing on the saddle of the wind.
The sky has a mission in every direction,
and in this place let your lifting begin.

for Wendy Erd

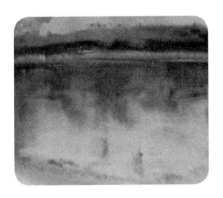

ONE

SITTING IN THE DARK

I am related to light.
Even nights I sit by a pond
that gathers the darkness into its arms,
where even the reeds lie still.

What is it I come here to know?
Some questions take forever to ask.
In water the moon casts her net
and the heart lies tangled in light.

In these moments
what is at stake?
Of darkness and light
what cousins will the soul make?

I am related to light.

THE MYTH MAKERS

Most of me was born here in a kitchen
where grandmother danced in straw shoes
and blessed me with her spatula, "To appease
the Chinese gods," she said, "and keep
your breasts from falling." As summer
thickened in the yard, we planted shamrocks
and practiced ESP. "I swear on Jesus, gin,
and the Union Jack that Winston Churchill
will come back." In the loose map of black
tea leaves she saw me walking backward
in a gown before the Queen. "You'll be
a Windsor—don't ever marry
a Catholic." Her yellow hands
greased the lamb with oil, while holding
a lit cigarette. I could not help
but hope, the gray ash turning red
as jewels tumbled from the air.
She had no breasts or teeth, and orange peel
withered on the stove, as she blew
her vapor rings and veiled
my flesh in smoke. Now,

my father's dead and seven stitches
seal my breast. In my kitchen, no man
views a new moon through the glass.
Last night my mother called.
My ex-fiancée shot himself.
He was Catholic, and fond of words
like "banshee" and "betrothed,"
I make soda bread, and mark the crust
with soil. I live

where the earth is always cold,
and floatplanes in a headwind
break a trail across the sky.
My neighbor claims Aurora has a song.
I haven't heard it yet. But lucky, yes,
to be awake as night unravels
into red. Perhaps we're made
of feather, thread, and storms,
but with winter almost over
I lay my faith in simple chores.
The stove is full of coals, and summer
was a season of the wasp. I shovel out
the ash, smear citrus
on the kitchen glass, and love
the stubborn blood and dead wings
as they dissolve in morning light.

FOUND

Grania's crate,
Large as a hope chest or small child's coffin.

Just an ordinary box, camouflaged by camp
Gear and cast-off teacups. Brimming

To its cedar plank lip; letters and her poems
Earmarked with my name and tears so old

They petrified the page with rings of rage
And signs of old growth. I shake it

Like a gift; hear paper chafe its
Thin yellow skin; make music

With the rattle of old bone pens.
Note after note, dust rising like a shout

From just buried ash,
Her breath ascends through ribs

Of shadow on the wall. I sing her in,
I swallow her strength,

And the smell of old books
Falls through me

Like sunlight
Or memory

Of Grania uncoiling her hair.

for Beatrice Elizabeth Patricia Cornwall

THE STONE HARVESTERS

I want a poem
from the stone.
I know it's there.
I heard it as a child
when Grandpa
dragged the heel of his lame leg
across the pavement.

It happened in a wheat field.
He was eight,
his foot
caught beneath a blade,
while tendons snapped
and words died out
like cement forgets the rain.
The harvest
continued on.

They say he shook
without a sound,
eyes white
as the pupils of a marble man.
And though he tried to speak again,
it seemed that pebbles filled his mouth.
I didn't know him.
He was hard
to understand.

But he showed me pictures once,
of a trip he made to Italy,
and sent a book
about an artist
who found men
inside of stone.

We buried him.
He wanted me
to carve the plaque.
And now I want the words
inside his stone.

for Fredrick Dobson

Isaac
will not go to mass.
He is deaf,
and no one there
can speak in sign.
When I return,
he is waiting in the garden
stringing Froot Loops on a vine.
I ask him,
"Are you making beads?"
He signs,
"No. I make a rosary
of weeds."

for William Stafford

MEDITATIONS ON BEETHOVEN

The road
to unreachable sound.

And proof the heart has
for its own set of ears.

A pond
where moonlight makes noise.

What silence sings
in deaf, bruised boys.

SESTINA: THE SIXTH DAY

Flour sifts the way a day
falls. In this life
and another, a woman is baking in a window, one eye
measuring yeast, a second instructing the sun,
who is her firstborn, a little man,
thinking of fresh bread and heaven.

"Is flour the dust of Heaven?"
The Gruel Dough ripens all day
and so death leavens in a man.
Clay bowl, linen cloth, rising life.
A belly blooming on the shelf, while the sun
cluttered kitchen bears memory, in a boy's eye.

And shadow brings evening to a woman's eye.
At the second rise, she proofs the dough for heaven
in a scorched pan buttered by sun.
Flawed hands test the work of one summer day.
Her dough springs back, and a resurrected life
shapes bread and rolls and a wafer man.

A boy opening the stove becomes a man.
Rubbing sea salt from his eye,
he thinks about eternal life
and what he knows of Heaven.
There must be bread, and one long day
with so much light, there is no need for sun.

And twilight brings manna from the sun.
The loaf is done, and coriander and honey a psalm in the mouth of a man.
A boy, full of bread, lies sleeping in the wild grass. The lamp is lit, another day
labors through the sieve of eternity. A mother's eye
is a covenant with shadow and the grain of heaven.
She craves the bread of angels and reads the book of life.

In this kitchen, a boy's life
began. Now, he is dreaming of the sun.
Crumbs are swept from the table in heaven
and frost blossoms in the field around a man.
As the moon rises in his mother's eye,
the sun is orphaned in the sky to seek another day.

What is kneaded in a day rises through a life.
A boy's eye loves summer and crust the color of sun.
When a man's bread sounds hollow, the labor of heaven and morning is done.

for Emily, who had no children,
and my mother, who did.

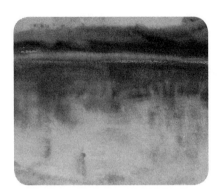

TWO

THE MOON AFTER ALL

you don't ask
but there it is
her song
every black night
the bone of solitude
sticks in your throat.

the moon after all
in perfect accompaniment
her lone note
risen from the windpipe of dusk

that hour severed
from morning
from
night.

FISH WIFE

What's the use
In being jealous of the sea?
She's a constant flirt; dark
Promise of seduction
Beneath her whitecapped skirt.

IDENTIFYING A HARBOR WITCH

First you must be a woman
who wakes by the sea.

    All men speak of you,
    they say your heart's
    in hibernation. In winter
    you soak your skin in sea,
    sleep at harbor's edge,
    become a piece of wood
    so petrified they can't
    see your growth. They hope
    you have no feeling left.
    When they sail away, weave
    seaweed through your hair.
    Make braids of jealousy. Crush
    bull kelp with your heel, when
    held by men in sun
    its bulb promises warm light.

    This will begin with a man
    who gives you eight stones
    from a shore called Desire
    where the sun is always rising.
    Each one has steeped so long
    in water dyed by dawn,
    that they are streaked with sunrise;
    especially when emerging
    from the moist clasp of a wave.
    He will give them to you the first
    morning you make love; one
    for each day you spent
    together. He will leave
    them tracking across your white
    sheets like the print of a wild animal
    on a thin skin of snow.

When it is understood
that he is never coming back,
you will swim to a frigid
coast you know and become this
woman who wakes by the sea. He
will fear you behind him,
rattling eight dawns in a bag,
cursing his name with the hiss
of each day you sink in the sea.

You will be a woman charmed
By the fire of his stones.

for Virginia Woolf

PURSUIT

We are creatures made for joy; if only we know how to reach.
—JAMES DICKEY, in a letter to Ann Sexton

On the nightstand;
tea, stale,
and coins he forgot.
Above the white mug
I cup my hand;
no steam,
no spice lifting
like scent from skin.

Breath is visible
in the coldest air.
Children clutch it,
want
with mittened hands,
to pluck it
hot
from the air
like an egg.

We are born chasing touch—
its brief and fragile heat.

THIRST

Kissing tulips, I
enter again your
indigo breath. My
tongue covets yours,
hovers

Kept and free and blessed. How
easily
nectar weeps. I
drink, lips
rabid for a smudge of bliss. The
ink of blossoms
coats my mouth. You
keep this color in your breath.

acrostic for Keith

PASSAGE

After you're done . . . what is there left
for you to confront but the great simplicities?
—STANLEY KUNITZ

You go. I gather the last
Of your exotic warmth; Moroccan
Mint tea lukewarm in the cup.
Even your spoon is no comfort—
My tongue in the center
Of its cold, hollow heart.

HAIR

You send a picture to your mother
and she writes back asking,
"Why did you shave your head?"
"What church do you go to now?"
And you remember that everyone but her
has seen you this naked before.

So you tell her about an old woman
you saw on the subway. The one
you thought had been a dancer
from the turned out way she walked
and the way she wouldn't
let her bruises show.
She didn't walk the way you thought
a beaten woman would walk.
She took small, vibrant steps,

still steps that barely moved.
Just enough space between joints
to get her from here to there
without shaking bones loose
or letting out the music inside.

Grace without sound.
When you asked her,
because it seemed important to know,
she told you that's her name.
Her full name.
Grace Without Sound.

And you tell your mother
it reminded you
of being picked up from ballet,
going home,

sitting on daddy's knee
while he pulled with a comb
and said "Princess, you're good,
but your body is wrong."
And you tell your mother
the woman's hair was perfect.
Pulled tight in a tail
that reached down her back,
hung black between her legs;
it was the only thing about her
that swung a little free. Even so

it pulled the skin at her temples,
made her eyes narrow
where they should have been wide.
It's hard to see the world
with hair held back that way.
And you tell your mother

you imagined the woman
brushing out her hair in the dark;
the way it would spark
blue like the lamp dad hung from the porch,
the one that killed flies quick
when they flew toward light,
though even that buzz
wasn't loud enough
to drown out the sound
of your mother knocked
senseless to the ground.

So you tell your mother
you thought these things and went home.
You looked in the mirror

and you knew what you wanted to see.
You wanted your locks
lying in the sink;
black finger marks on porcelain skin.

So you shaved your head.
It was raw for a while,
but now you like the way it chafes,
burns, breathes. Your shock
of held back rage.

for Zoeanne

VEHICLE

At daybreak I drove from home
to a place called Overlook.
The road was long and steep,
as it always is,
there were difficult corners,
as there always are,
and around each bend I said
"I want my fervor back."

Sometimes the heart
is an old blue car,
paint peeling,
garbage in the cup holder and no back bumper,
Skittles and coins between the seats.

And yet,
I reached the top
to watch sunlight blend with the wind,
and my heart, each cracked, unoiled part,
was fueled with inexplicable joy.

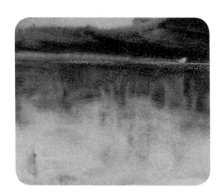

THREE

DEFINING PRIZE

(Webster's Collegiate Dictionary, *1976*)

1

"something offered . . . in contests of chance"
One summer,
after rape,
I found eight
four-leaf clovers.

2

"something taken by force"
I picked them.
I dried them.
I locked them
in a drawer.

3

"to estimate the value of (archaic)"
Back then,
at ten,
it was
enough.

4

"something exceptionally desired"
To hoard luck.
To guard luck
To think God
was making up.

WINTER HEART

White sack

caught in the black
dance of a dead tree.

Thin plastic skin
ripe with wind and light.

Blossom
flirting with decay,

angel
in a see-through dress,

egg
that wants a chance

to woo the numb to breath.

THE BLESSING END

Icicles melt,
their long wands
first filling up with light.
We break them off
to place the blessing end
inside our mouths.

Let's claim there's grace
for the dead who still have thirst,

toast now what grieves
and yet hosts mirth,

confess we live
and long for birth.

for the ice sculptor, Lyn Marie Naden

FRIEND

When I am with you, I belong
to the spontaneous chorus of all green things.
If I listen, your words are crystals
woven through wind. When we walk
talking in the black woods,
the end believes in beginning again.

WALK RECKLESSLY

In the smallest room in Alaska
we dream of a wider world.
There is so little space
there is only one good place to stand;
in front of an untrimmed window
that knows the mountain,
the neighbor, the world.
From here, there is no horizon.
Fog rolls up over its lip
so there is only a possible line. Yesterday,

outside this door,
the tsunami of a great silence.
Today, the echo of a boy
who swore he wouldn't write poetry,
then asked you how to spell *scar*.
I warn you about pushki.
The blister, the burn.
How broken leaves and blood
collide with skin and light.
A cow moose looks over her shoulder
at something we can't see.
A calf. A bear.
We are both hungry.

You open the door.
I watch you walk up the slim path,
move with ease and tenderness
among the toxic plants.
I follow.
Even though I have good balance,
I walk with my arms held wide.

for Kim Stafford, Kachemak Bay, Alaska

NEIGHBOR

(Kachemak Bay to Vietnam)

Each word is harbor for the next,
from your shore to mine
the sea says the same thing.
Let our days, be hand-painted plates
we pass among our friends—
a ladle lying empty by the sink,
the blue bowl heavy
as its compost overflows. We come,
like a bear to the meadow
where roe for the Buddha ripens in the grass.
As autumn leaves lay all God's tables,
roots toughen in the garden, drink sugar from the past.

MIRACLE

Midwinter, among
old-growth trees,
one shoot strays
toward the light.

What odds.
It isn't much.
Such room for dark
to play its part.

The gleam of green.
Faith, thaw,
Spring, sun;
they'll come again.

What mystery!
The tale itself
becomes enough.
I kneel to praise

what reaches up.

for Emily Dickinson

ROUGH DRAFTS

Earth and snow.
From the meeting of these great hands
we want some sound.
A clap. But there is nothing,
or the ebbing of some psalm
the heart has yet to learn.
This is the hardest kind of listening.
And who will care?
Most do not.
It doesn't matter.
It is all applause,
applause, applause.

How is it possible
to ask for more than that?

for Dorothy and William Stafford

FOUR

WHAT WHALES AND INFANTS KNOW

Beluga Point, Turnagain Arm, Alaska

A beluga rising
from the ocean's muddy depths
reshapes its head to make a sound
or take a breath.

I want to come

at air and light like this.
To make my heart
a white arc above the muck of certain days,
and from silence and strange air

send a song

to breach the surface
where what we need most
lives.

"What Whales and Infants Know" by Kim Cornwall
Beluga Point, Turnagain Arm, Chugach State Park, Alaska

AFTERWORD

The last poem is not the end of this book. Nor even, in a way, of Kim.

One summer afternoon weeks after Kim died, stark lonesome for her,
I jogged through a field of rose-violet fireweed. Suddenly Kim's poem
"What Whales and Infants Know" with its attributed location—Beluga
Point, Turnagain Arm, Alaska—landed like a small bird in my mind. I
felt sure the poem belonged on a sign at Beluga Point, a small rest stop
along the highway just south of Anchorage, a place perched between the
slant of great mountains and a shifting tidal sea.

The idea of a poem inhabiting a wild place wasn't new. Kim and I often talked of traveling together to the Methow River in Washington to read William Stafford's poems set on signs along the river valley. Two forest service employees approached Stafford in 1992 and asked him to write a series of poems that would reflect the landscape and spirit of the North Cascades, words that might stretch imaginations and spirits.

> Sometimes when the river is ice ask me / mistakes I have made.
> (William Stafford, "Ask Me," Methow River poems)

When I got home, I called Alaska's Department of Transportation. They referred me to Tom Harrison, the superintendent of Chugach State Park, a man taxed with the practicalities of overseeing five hundred thousand acres of wilderness and this particular pullout. Out of the blue I launched the idea.

Whatever positive forces there are in the world were poised and polished in that moment of receptivity. Tom said, *read it to me.* I read the poem. After a long pause he said, *Yes ... yes you are right. How can we make this happen?* How unlikely. How extraordinary. That small bird. Kim.

We needed a larger circle of support. A friend suggested I contact Charlotte Fox, then director of the Alaska State Council on the Arts. She knew of "What Whales and Infants Know." ASCA had selected this poem for a National Poetry Month mailer and invited GCI to include it along with their April phone bills. She belonged to the Friends of William Stafford. Charlotte was the perfect partner. Alaska State Parks donated sign expertise and a graphic artist. Family and friends donated funds. Two parks employees showed up with tools and set the sign in place. In May 2011 on a brilliant, windy day we dedicated the poem to tears and laughter, recordings of Beluga whales, tea and more poetry.

Claire LeClair, deputy director of Alaska State Parks, a lover of both parks and poetry, attended the dedication. Afterward Charlotte, Claire and I knew we had to continue. Unlikely partners as we were, we recognized a magic opportunity to work together to link people, wild places and poetry. The idea for Poems in Place, a three-year statewide project, was born.

Our dream was to choose parks in all seven districts of Alaska in which to place poems, paired with a piece of art, on permanent signs until we seeded our huge state with poetry available to all who happened upon them, by intent or by chance. A long embrace began, everyone we contacted said yes. With the promise inherent in unique collaborations, state parks, arts and humanity organizations, the Alaska Center for the Book and generous and diverse funders all rose to celebrate and support the idea. We gathered an insightful committee of poets and writers who helped imagine and guide the project and who judged, along with local parks advisors, the outpouring of poetry we received.

Kim would have loved the democracy of welcome. All Alaskans were invited to express their connection to a place that mattered to them. We sought poems that, as William Stafford once said, were "rooted in place and lifted to an idea." Over the course of three years we received more than a hundred submissions. Poems arrived from people in remote villages, from towns and cities. One poem was handwritten in prison. People who may never have written a poem before let a wild place sieve through them.

Now there are eleven poems set in state parks across Alaska. Kim's long reach launched a wide landscape of poetry, writers and uncommon readers. Wanderers-by happen upon poems in unsuspected places, by a bend along a northern river, near totem poles in southeast Alaska, on the edge of a remote lake in Bristol Bay, high on a hill by an abandoned mine. People who might never crack open a book of poetry, continue to stop, linger and find something that speaks to them there.

ACKNOWLEDGMENTS

I wish to thank the editors of the following publications in which these poems first appeared.

"The Blessing End," Kenai Peninsula Writers' Contest 2001, *Homer News*.

"Identifying a Harbor Witch," Fairbanks Arts Association Poetry Contest, 2003.

"Lungdhar (*Wind Flag*)," University of Alaska Anchorage/*Anchorage Daily News* Creative Writing Contest, 2004, honorable mention; *The Alaska Reader: Voices from the North*, edited by Anne Hanley and Carolyn Kremers (Golden, CO: Fulcrum, 2005).

"The Myth Makers," University of Alaska Anchorage/*Anchorage Daily News* Creative Writing Contest, 2007, first place, Open to the Public Poetry and Editor's Choice.

"What Whales and Infants Know," University of Alaska, Explorations 1999 and Wilderness, Wildlands and People: A Partnership for the Planet 2008.

Kim and Spunky.
Celebrating Canada Day July 1, 2005
Outside her home, Fairbanks, Alaska.